Record Collector's Fact Book

Vol. I
45 RPM
1952-1965

by
Chuck Brigermann

Published by:

Disc Publishing
3531 Oxwed Court
Westminster, MD 21157

Distributed to bookstores by:
Liberty Publishing Company
50 Scott Adam Road
Cockeysville, MD 21030

Design/Typography by Winterhawk Graphics, Inc.
13816 Jarrettsville Pike
Phoenix, MD 21131

Printing by Universal Lithographers
10626 York Road
Cockeysville, Maryland 21030

Library of Congress #82-73474
ISBN 0-89709-037-3

Manufactured in USA

This book is dedicated to one of the premiere record collectors in the world. Without his help and resources this book would have been nearly impossible. Thanks to my good friend Val Shively.

INTRODUCTION - PLEASE READ

The purpose of this book is to aid in the identification of original, first press, 45 RPM records. The proliferation of the record collecting hobby has created an increased demand for not only rare and obscure records, but many of the "top 40" hits also. Many collectors, especially those at the novice level, do not have any basis to work from in differentiating first presses from reproductions, reissues, and subsequent presses. On the following pages we have attempted to provide this basis.

There already exist many fine books dealing with prices and discographies, and no attempt will be made to duplicate this information here. Of the thousands of labels in existence, about five hundred were chosen because of their collector interest, difficulty in determining first press, or the availability of reproduction pressings. This volume contains facts on approximately seventy labels. An attempt to document every label in a single volume would have kept much of the information out of the collector's hands for too long a period. Listed on page IX are all the labels to be included in this and future volumes. Any accurate information regarding these labels will always be appreciated and should be sent directly to the publisher.

This volume contains a photo section to be used in conjunction with label descriptions. Within each description will be information on label design variations and a complete list of known reproductions. Please keep in mind that label design changes were almost never 100% complete at a specific record number. Different pressing plants, a record's popularity, and even old labels lying around, account for discs appearing with labels that were discontinued even years before. Two fine examples of this are: "What'd I Say" by Ray Charles (Atlantic 2031) appearing on a yellow label with no fan (in reality a dj copy) and "Peek A Boo" by the Cadillacs on the early brown print label (Josie 846). There are, of course, instances where companies used more than one label style at the same time. In this case each one is considered original and scarcity usually dictates demand and value.

Reproductions usually present a problem equal in magnitude to the quality used in producing them. Some are extremely good and almost have to be compared to an original for detection. The most common justification for reproductions is that they provide the collector with a record that he or she might otherwise never own. This is fine if the record is never misrepresented as an original. A simple indication that everyone could recognize in the dead wax would have helped prevent any future rip off. This method was used by a couple of conscientious people. By putting the date or other information in the dead wax they have provided the record, and its sound, to the collector, without providing a potential money maker to the unscrupulous. Please note that some of the detection tips, although a reasonable guarantee of originality, do not always apply to each and every original that was pressed. For instance an original may have been machine stamped with the word Sheldon. This does not necessarily mean every original was machine stamped with the word Sheldon.

As a final suggestion, know who you are dealing with whenever possible. Unfortunately there are very few true record experts in the entire country, but with the expansion of the hobby, and continued education throught the efforts of these experts, we may all become experts one day. A special thanks to these people...

ACKNOWLEDGEMENTS

The two people that have addresses listed along with their names are highly recommended, reputable record dealers.

Dave Antrell

Phil Chaney

Goldmine Magazine

Alan Lee

Victor Pearlin
PO Box 199A
Greendale Station
Worcestor, MA 01606

Charles Reinhart

Don Riswick

Val Shively
Box B
Havertown, PA 19082

Bob Synder

Bob Volturno

I would also like to thank the following people for providing label photographs:

Doc Hersperger
Bob Hruz
Artie Kauffman
Mike Sanford

GENERAL INFORMATION

The word reproduction used in this book refers to fairly exact copies of originals in both label design and the actual recording. These are also sometimes referred to as boots or bootlegs even though this term normally refers to material previously unrecorded. Records previously unrecorded as originals are not included in this book. The lack of originality in these cases should be obvious.

A number of machine stamped symbols will be referred to in this book. MR with a circle around it, Sheldon, Audio Matrix, etc., are figures used by people involved in the manufacture of a particular record. As stated in the introduction, the appearance of these symbols in the dead wax is a good indication of originality, but originals of the same record may exist without this symbol because of multiple pressings. A hand written delta symbol (triangle), followed by a number, is also usually a good indication of an original. Hand written dates in the wax, much later than when the record was originally produced, are an indication of a reproduction. The letters CS or the separate number 340 are also good indications of a reproduction. The correct label, and one of good quality, are two more things to compare. During the 50's there was a transition period where 45's and 78's were both being produced. As a result many 45's were pressed with the number 45 as part of the information in the dead wax. This is helpful because many (not all) of the reproductions left this out. A final point worth noting is the practice of machine stamping the numbers in the dead wax. This was done by some companies, and with the exception of a few records, is an excellent indication of an original. The above information, coupled with the knowledge that a particular reproduction exists, should enable you to identify most records.

Every effort was made to list all existing reproductions, but there are surely a few that will have been missed. Some specifications on originals are also missing because it is impossible to examine every variation of every record from each company. The information that is given should provide nearly everyone with something helpful.

Most of the smaller labels, or labels with one or two significant releases, will only have a write-up detailing pertinent information and a list of reproductions, if any. Larger labels, or where necessary, a specifications section will contain known variations and other facts. The delta number pressings will be noted if they offer some significance.

MASTER LIST OF LABELS

AARDELL
AARON
ABBEY
ABC PAR
ABNER
ACADEMY
ACE
ACME
ADONIS
AFO
AFTER HOURS
ALADDIN
ALJON
AL KING
ALLEN
ALL STAR
ALPINE
AMP 3
ANDREA
ANGLE TONE
APOLLO
APT
ARGO
ARVEE
ARWIN
ATCO
ATLANTIC
ATLAS
ATOMIC
AUDICON
AUDIO

BACK BEAT
BAND BOX
BANG
BARONET
BATON
BAYFRONT
BEACON
BEE
BEECH
BETHLEHEM
BETTA
B&F
BIG
BIG HOWDY
BIG TOP
BLAST
BLUE HORIZON
BLUE LAKE
BLUES BOYS
KINGDOM
BOBBIN
BOLD
BOSS
BOULEVARD
BOW
BRUCE
BRUNSWICK
BUCCANEER
BULLSEYE

CADENCE
CALICO
CALO
CAL WEST
CAMEO
CANDIX
CANDLELIGHT
CAPITOL
CAPRI
CAPRICE
CARNIVAL
CAROUSEL
CARVER
CASA GRANDE
CASH
CASINO
CAT
CELESTE
CENTAUR
CENTRAL
CHALLENGE
CHAMPAGNE
CHANCE
CHANCELLOR
CHARIOT
CHART
CHECKER
CHERRY
CHESAPEAKE
CHESS
CHEX
CHICAGO
CHIEF
CHOCK FULL OF HITS
CINDY
CIRCUS
CLASS
CLAUWELL
CLIX
CLOCK
CLUB 51
COBRA
COED
COLONIAL
COLPIX
COLUMBIA
COMBO
COMET
COMPANION
CORAL
COUGAR
COUSINS
C&R
CREST
CROSSROADS
CROSSTOWN
CROWN
CUB
CYCLONE

D
DANICE
DAPT
DAVIS
DAWN
DCP
DEAN
DECATUR
DECCA
DEE DEE
DEL FI
DELUXE
DEMON
DERBY
DFS
DIG

DISNEYLAND
DMG
DOLPHIN
DOLTON
DOME
DON
DONNA
DOOTO(NE)
DORE
DO RE MI
DOT
DRAGON
DREEM
DREXEL
DRUMMOND
DUB
DUEL
DUKE
DUNES
DU WELL
DYNAMIC

EARL
EAST WEST
EBB
EKKO
ELDO
ELGEY
ELMAR
ELMONT
ELMOR
EMBER
EMGE
EMPIRE
EMPRESS
END
ENTERPRISE
ENTRA
EPIC
ERA
ESSEX
EVERLAST
EXCELLO
EXCELSIOR

FALCON
FAME
FARGO
FEDERAL
FEEBEE
FELCO
FELICE
FIDELITY
FIRE
FLAIR
FLASH
FLICK
FLIP
FORD
FOREVER
FORTUNE
FRATERNITY
FURY
FUTURE

GALLIANT
GAME
GAME TIME
GARDENA
GARPAX
GARRETT
GATEWAY
GAYNOTE
GC
GEE
GEM
GENERAL
GIBRALTER
GIGI
GILCO
GLORY
G&M
GOLDISC
GONE
GOOD
GORDY
GOTHAM
GRAND
GREAT LAKES
GROOVE
GSP
GUYDEN
G&W

HARLEM
HAVEN
HERALD
HICKORY
HIGHLAND
HI PO
HI Q
HOLIDAY
HOLLYWOOD
HOWARD
HUB
HUDSON
HULL
HUNT
HUT
HYTONE

IMPALA
IMPERIAL
IRMA
IRVANNE
ISLAND
IVY

JAGUAR
JALYNNE
JAMIE
JAVA
JAX
JAY DEE
JDS
JEANNIE
JEM
JERDEN
JE WEL
J&G
JIN
JOB
JOEY
JOHNSON
JORDAN
JOSIE
JOYCE
J&S
JUBILEE
JUDD
JUNIOR
JVB

KAPP
KAPPA
KAY
KAYBO
K&C
KEEN
KELIT
KELWAY
KENT
KHOURYS

KICKS
KING
KIRSHNER
KLIFF
KOKO

LAKE
LAMA
LAMP
LANA
LANDA
LAURIE
LECAM
LEE
LEE TONE
LEGRAND
LESLEY
LIBERTY
LIDO
LITE
LITTLE
LLOYDS
LO FI
LOMA
LONDON
LOVE
LUCKY
LUNA
LUNIVERSE
LYNNE

MADISON
MAGNET
MAGNIFICENT
MAINLINE
MALA
MAMBO
MARK X
MARLIN
MARSHALL
MAR VEE
MARVEL
MARVELLO
MASCOT
MAY
MAYHAMS
MELBA
MEMPHIS
MERCURY
MERMAID
MGM

MIDA
MIDDLE TONE
MILESTONE
MILMART
MILO
MINIT
MINT
MIRASONIC
MIST
MJC
MODERN
MOHAWK
MONA LEE
MONEY
MONUMENT
MOTOWN
MUNICH
MUSIC CITY
MUSICNOTE
MUSITRON
MUSTANG
MZ

NANC
NATIONAL
NATURAL
NEIL
NEPTUNE
NEWPORT
NIX
NO MAR
NOTE
NUKAT

OASIS
OJ
OKEH
OLD TOWN
ONYX
ORIGINAL SOUND

PA GO GO
PARADISE
PARIS
PARK
PARKWAY
PARROT
PEACOCK
PEE DEE
PERRI
PET

PHILLES
PING
PLA BACK
PLANET
PLAYGROUND
PLUS
PORT
PORWIN
POST
POWER
PREMIUM
PRESTIGE
PRO
PROMO

QUALITY

RAINBOW
RAMA
RANDY
RANSON
RAYS
R&B
RCA
REC. IN HOLLYWOOD
RED ROBIN
RED TOP
REED
REGENT
RENDEZVOUS
REPUBLIC
RESERVE
RHYTHM
RIBBON
RIC
RICHIE
RIFT
RIKI
RIVIERA
ROBBINS
ROBIN
RO CAL
ROCKET
ROCKIN
ROCK IT
ROLLIN
ROME
RONEL
ROULETTE
RPM
RULU
RUST –

RUST

SABINA
SABRE
SABRINA
SAFARI
SAGA
SALEM
SAMPSON
SAN
SANTA CRUZ
SARA
SATELLITE
SATURN
SAVOY
SAXONY
SCARLET
SCEPTER
SCORE
SCORPIO
SEGWAY
SELECTIVE
SEVEN ELEVEN
SEVILLE
SGC
SHAD
SHELL
SHERYL
SHIMMY
SHIP
SHOWTIME
SIMS
SINGULAR
SMASH
SNAG
SNAP
SOUTHERN
SPACE
SPARE
SPARK
SPECIALTY
SPIN
SPQR
SPRING
SRC
STANDORD
STARDAY
STAR MAKER
STATES
STEAMBOAT
STORM
STRATE 8
STREAMLINE
STUDIO
SUDDEN
SUE
SUN
SUNCOAST
SUNNY
SURE
SURF
SURPRISE
SUSSEX
SWAMI
SWAN
SWINGIN
SWINGTIME
SYMBOL
SYRUP BUCKET

TAG
TAMARA
TAMLA
TAMPA
TANDEN
TAURUS
TEE KAY
TEENAGE
TEL
TENDER
TETRA
TIARA
TICO
TIME
TIMELY
TIMES SQUARE
TIN PAN ALLEY
TIP TOP
TOLLIE
TOPIX
TOWER
TREAT
TRESS
TRI BORO
TRIPLE D
TRIPLE X
TROMMERS
TUXEDO
20TH FOX
TWIST
TWO MIKES

UC
UNART
UNIQUE
UNITED
UNITED ART
UNIVERSAL
USA

VAL
VALIANT
VALMOR
VAL UE
VARBEE
VEE JAY
VEGA
VEKO
VERVE
VERY RECORD
VEST
VESTA
VIK
VIOLET
VITA
VULCAN

WAND
WANGER
WARNER
WARNER BR.
WARWICK
WATTS
WAY OUT
WHIPPET
WHITE ROCK
WHIZ
WING
WINLEY
WINN
WONDER
WORTHY

X
X L
XYZ
XTRA

YALE
YOUR COPY

FOREWORD

With record collecting fast becoming a recognized hobby much the same as stamps, coins, trains, comic books, etc., there's a growing need for collectors to be aware of the difference between first pressings, second pressings, bootlegs or counterfeits. A counterfeit is an unlawful reproduction of an original recording that looks like an original. A bootleg is not always on the original label, however, in this book consider the word bootleg to mean counterfeit, since the boots listed were in most cases photographed from the labels of originals. I'm not against bootlegs as long as they are sold or traded as such. It's my opinion that if bootlegs hadn't come into the hobby as they did in the early and mid 60's, R & B collecting wouldn't be where it is today. It wouldn't have made it out of the 60's. Boots made the sound available to the collectors at a fraction of the cost of an original.

Since so many people are selling records today through publications like *Goldmine* or private set sale or auction lists, you can't always assume that if a record is advertised as being original, it is. Many people just don't know the difference. So if you're Involved with collecting original labels, this book will help you determine first pressings on the labels listed.

Hope you enjoy it and find it useful.

Val Shively
R & B Records
Box B
Havertown, PA 19083

TABLE OF CONTENTS

ABNER/FALCON

This series began on the Falcon label, but because of a conflict with a company of the same name, the label was changed to Abner. Falcon used records numbered 1000 thru 1013. Record 1013 was also issued by Abner, and the releases continued thru 1037. The label design remained the same throughout with the exception of the name change. The reproductions on Falcon are distinguished by the lack of label detail especially in the area of the bird feathers.

REPRODUCTIONS

1006	**Falcons**	Now That It's Over
1013	**Jerry Butler**	For Your Precious Love (On the Falcon label)

ACE

This label is not to be confused with the New York label of the same name. The 8000 series was issued after the take over by Vee Jay, and this is reflected in the slightly different label.

SPECIFICS

500 thru 504 — Black label.

505 thru 527 — yellow label without Vee Jay on the side.

528 thru 553 — white with the number at the bottom.

554 thru 672 — mostly white with the number on the right, some purple.
575, 576, and 584 exist on a purple label.

8001 — begins yellow label with Vee Jay.

REPRODUCTIONS

530	Huey Smith	Rockin' Pneumonia
534	Supremes	Just For You And I
545	Huey Smith	Don't You Just Know It
546	Jimmy Clanton	Just A Dream
554	Frankie Ford	Sea Cruise
8001	Jimmy Clanton	Venus In Blue Jeans

ALADDIN

Aladdin had a 100 and 200 series in the forties. These, as well as the beginning of the 3000 series, were all 78 RPM. Many of the original recordings are delta pressings and the prefix 45-AL is used extensively.

SPECIFICS

3055 thru 3259 — blue label.

3260 thru 3399 — blue or maroon label.
3398 also appears on a purple label and the later black label.

3400 — begins black label.

REPRODUCTIONS

3031	Robins	Don't Like The Way You're Doing (Original is 78 only)
3085	Five Keys	With A Broken Heart (Original unknown on 45 RPM)
3113	Five Keys	It's Christmas Time
3118	Five Keys	Yes Sir That's My Baby
3119	Five Keys	Darling (Original unknown on 45 RPM)
3123	Balladiers	Forget Me Not
3127	Five Keys	Red Sails In The Sunset
3131	Five Keys	Mistakes

3136	Five Keys	I Hadn't Anyone Til You
3158	Five Keys	I Cried For You
3167	Five Keys	Can't Keep From Crying
3170	Sha Weez	No One To Love Me
3173	Shirley & Lee	Baby
3175	Five Keys	There Ought To Be A Law
3182	Five Keys	I'll Always Be In Love With You
3190	Five Keys	These Foolish Things
3197	Amos Milburn	What Can I Do
3204	Five Keys	Teardrops In Your Eyes
3210	Bachelors	Can't Help Loving You
3214	Five Keys	My Saddest Hour
3228	Five Keys	Someday Sweetheart
3245	Five Keys	Deep In My Heart
3247	Jets	I'll Hide My Tears
3259	Dodgers	You Make Me Happy
3263	Five Keys	My Love
3267	Feathers	Johnny Darling
3274	Four Jacks	This Is My Last Affair
3275	Aladdins	Remember
3277	Feathers	I Need A Girl
3298	Aladdins	I Had A Dream Last Night
3312	Five Keys	Story Of Love
3314	Aladdins	All My Life
3324	Flairs	Be Cool My Love
3325	Shirley & Lee	Let The Good Times Roll
3338	Shirley & Lee	I Feel Good
3347	Jivers	Ray Pearl
3377	Bob Ehret	Stop The Clock
3384	Big T Tyler	King Kong
3391	Velvetones	I Found My Love
3393	Jayhawks	Everyone Should Know
3398	Thurston Harris	Little Bitty Pretty One
3401	Sharps	What Will I Gain
3415	Thurston Harris	Be Babe Leba
3436	Spotlighters	Whisper

AMP3

The reproduction on the AMP3 label, number 2115, "One Summer Night" by the Dandleers (Danleers on Mercury) should have "Distributed By Mercury Record Corp." across the top of the label, and the number is machine stamped in the dead wax.

REPRODUCTIONS ———

132	Empires	Zippety Zip
2115	Dandleers	One Summer Night

APT

APT primarily used one label style for all of their recordings. The obvious exception to this is their biggest hit, "Little Star" by the Elegants. The plain black label version of this is an additional pressing.

SPECIFICS ———

25001 thru 25080 — multicolor label.
25005 also released on a plain black label with silver print.

25081 — begins two tone label.

REPRODUCTIONS ———

25005	Elegants	Little Star (plain black label)
25046	Limelites	One Week From Today

ARGO

SPECIFICS

5250 thru 5281 — gray and black label with a ship in the background.

5382 thru 5405 — black label with vertical Argo. Note the overlap below.

5361 — begins tan label.

REPRODUCTIONS

5286	**Orbits**	Who Are You
5309	**Eddie Fontaine**	Nothin' Shakin'
5340	**Mel Robbins**	Save It
5386	**Students**	I'm So Young
5405	**Sensations**	Let Me In (black label)

ATCO

The first ATCO releases, 6050 thru 6090, were on a maroon label with gold print. Many of these have been released again on the later yellow and white label. Even though the yellow and white label began with 6091 and continued throughout the ATCO series, there was a minor change around 1967, the inclusion of 1841 Broadway at the bottom of the label. Records released prior to number 6462 do not have this address if they are originals. Anything with the complete address before this number is a second press. ATCO wrote a small AT in the dead wax and the reproductions do not have this. The AT is written alone in the wax and is not part of the record number.

SPECIFICS

6050 thru 6090 — maroon label.

6091 thru 6461 — yellow and white label without 1841 Broadway.

REPRODUCTIONS

6052	Royal Jokers	Stay here
6057	Pearls	Shadows Of Love
6087	Coasters	Young Blood
6088	Flyers	My Only Desire
6116	Coasters	Yakety Yak
6117	Bobby Darin	Splish Splash
6127	Bobby Darin	Queen Of The Hop
6132	Coasters	Charlie Brown
6140	Bobby Darin	Dreamlover
6147	Bobby Darin	Mac The Knife
6158	Bobby Darin	Beyond The Sea
6302	Beatles	Sweet Georgia Brown
6308	Beatles	Ain't She Sweet

ATLANTIC

Although Atlantic began with number 851, this and many other early releases were not issued on a 45. Many of the 45's on the yellow and black label were reissued, but are easily identified by the small fan on the left of the label. The originals did not have this fan. A similar situation exists on the red and black label. The first issues on red and black did not have the fan, but records that remained popular after the fan was added were pressed on the then current red and black label with the fan.

SPECIFICS

914 thru 1083 — yellow and black label, no fan.
914, 919, and 932 are the only known 45's prior to 933.
936, 937, 938, 940, 941, 942, and 947 are not known to exist on a 45.
1083 was issued originally on both the yellow and the red labels.

1083 thru 2136 — red and black label, no fan.
1156 not known to exist on a 45.
2031 on the earlier yellow and black label is a dj copy.

2137 — begins red and black with fan.

REPRODUCTIONS

889	Delta Rhythm Boys	The Laughs On Me
934	Clovers	Skylark
938	Cardinals	Shouldn't I Know (Original unknown on 45 RPM)
981	Diamonds	A Beggar For Your Kisses
1020	Professor Long Hair	In The Night
1045	Johnny Jones	Hoy Hoy
1137	Dean Beard	On My Mind Again (DJ)
1158	Clyde McPhatter	Rock & Cry
2025	Drifters	There Goes My Baby
2119	LaVern Baker	Voodoo Voodoo
2237	Drifters	Under the Boardwalk

AUDICON

The plain red label shown in the photo section with AUDICON in ¼" print is a first press. Other sizes and/or spacings for 102 are later pressings.

SPECIFICS

101 thru 105 – plain red.

105 – begins orange, black and white label. Note 105 comes both ways.

REPRODUCTIONS

None

BACK BEAT

There are no known reproductions on the Back Beat label, but reissues of earlier material were repressed on the red label.

SPECIFICS

500 thru 530 — white/blue/green label.

531 — begins red drumstick label.

REPRODUCTIONS

None.

BRUNSWICK

The Lennon Sisters appeared on the first Brunswick release in the 55000 series. Quite a few reproductions exist, but are easily detected because of the lack of a machine stamped number in the dead wax.

SPECIFICS

55000 thru 55166 — maroon label.

55167 thru 55250 — orange label.

55250 — begins black label.

REPRODUCTIONS

55009	**Crickets**	That'll Be The Day
55035	**Crickets**	Oh Boy
55039	**Peanuts Wilson**	Cast Iron Arm

55052	Jackie Wilson	To Be Loved
55053	Crickets	Maybe Baby
55066	Billy Harlan	I Wanna Bop
55072	Crickets	Think It Over
55087	Jaytones	Gasoline
55089	Youngtones	Come On Baby
55094	Crickets	It's So Easy
55105	Jackie Wilson	Lonely Teardrops
55115	Lou Giordano	Stay Close To Me
55121	Jackie Wilson	That's Why
55130	Waylon Jennings	Jole Blon
55136	Jackie Wilson	I'll Be Satisfied
55166	Jackie Wilson	Night
55221	Jackie Wilson	The Greatest Hurt
55336	Jackie Wilson	Higher And Higher

CAMEO

Cameo records began this series in 1957 with "Old Enough To Know" by Arlene DeMarco.

SPECIFICS

100 thru 178 — orange label primarily.
121, 125, and 126 exist on yellow.

179 — begins red and black label.

REPRODUCTIONS

123	Cameos	Merry Christmas
171	Bobby Rydell	Wild One
179	Bobby Rydell	Volare
270	Little Cheryl	Heaven Only Knows

CAPITOL

Records produced by Capitol prior to number 3311, that are within the scope of this book, are on a purple label with a large (about ½") Capitol logo at the top. Other styles and changes are detailed below. Second presses exist on the yellow and orange swirl label, and can be detected by the addition of "A Subsidiary Of Capitol Industries" at the bottom of the label. This wording did not exist on originals until about 1969. None of the original Beatle recordings on the yellow and orange swirl label should have this additional wording. It should also be pointed out that after record number 5999, Capitol started over with number 2000 instead of going to 6000 which was already being used for the Starline series.

SPECIFICS

3310 and before — purple label with large Capitol logo at the top.

3311 thru 4290 — purple label with small Capitol logo at the top.
A few numbers up to 3450 appear with the large logo.

4291 thru 4674 — purple label with the Capitol logo on the left.
4671 appears on the yellow and orange swirl also.

4675 — begins orange and yellow swirl.

REPRODUCTIONS

3450	**Gene Vincent**	Be Bop A Lula
3763	**Gene Vincent**	Lotta Lovin'
3839	**Gene Vincent**	Dance To The Bop
3966	**Johnny Otis**	Willie And The Hand Jive
4128	**Rob Roys**	Pizza Pie

The remainder of the reproductions are all Beatle records, and all suffer from a lack of label detail (small print is not sharp). In addition, originals with the exception of 5407 and 5555 were machine stamped with a small triangle which can be used for additional verification. 5407 had a machine stamped number.

5112	Beatles	I Want To Hold Your Hand
5150	Beatles	Can't Buy Me Love
5222	Beatles	A Hard Days Night
5234	Beatles	I'll Cry Instead
5235	Beatles	If I Fell
5255	Beatles	Matchbox
5327	Beatles	I Feel Fine
5371	Beatles	Eight Days A Week
5407	Beatles	Ticket To Ride
5476	Beatles	Help
5498	Beatles	Yesterday
5555	Beatles	We Can Work It Out
5587	Beatles	Nowhere Man
5651	Beatles	Paperback Writer
5715	Beatles	Yellow Submarine
5810	Beatles	Penny Lane
5964	Beatles	All You Need Is Love
2056	Beatles	Hello Goodbye
2138	Beatles	Lady Madonna

CHALLENGE

Some of the Challenge label styles had the initials GA at the top. This is just a bit of vanity by the owner, Gene Autry.

SPECIFICS

1001 thru 1007 — dark blue label.

1008 thru 1013 — light blue with Challenge written in an arc.

1013 thru 1018 — maroon label.
1013 also appeared on a medium blue label with red print.

59000 thru 59106 — maroon label.

9107 thru 9205 — green label, Dist. By Warner Bros. Records.

59205 thru 59278 — green label.

59279 — begins black label.

REPRODUCTIONS

1016 Champs — Tequila

CHANCELLOR

The initial Chancellor label was pink with some variation in the depth of the color. Since there is no apparent pattern to this variation, information is not included. All are originals.

SPECIFICS

1000 thru 1036 — pink label.
1031 appears as a double horizontal line variation.

1035 — begins black label.
1036 as noted above appears on pink also.

REPRODUCTIONS

1031 Frankie Avalon — Venus

CHECKER

SPECIFICS

750 thru 800 — maroon label with a silver web top.
752, 753, 756 and 757 are not known to exist on a 45.

801 thru 876 — same as above with the addition of Record Co. in the underscore of Checker.

877 thru 1050 — maroon label with Checker written vertically.

1051 thru 1104 — maroon label with vertical Checker or blue label with checkers across the top.

1105 thru 1120 — maroon or red label with vertical Checker or blue label with checkers.

1120 thru 1135 — maroon label or blue label with or without checkers.

1136 — begins blue label without checkers except as noted above.

REPRODUCTIONS

767	Little Walter	Don't Have To Hunt No More
777	Elmore James	She Just Won't Do Right
782	Blue Jays	White Cliffs Of Dover
794	El Rays	Darling I Know
800	Teasers	How Could You Hurt Me So
807	Otis Spann	It Must Have Been The Devil
915	Flamingos	Whispering Stars
1120	Fontella Bass	Rescue Me
1121	G.L. Crockett	Did You Ever Love Somebody
1129	Bobby Moore	Searchin' For My Love

CHESS

SPECIFICS

1425 thru 1670 — blue label with silver top.

1671 thru 1798 — dark blue with Chess written vertically.

1799 thru 1840 — dark blue or multicolor label.

1841 — begins multicolor or black label, a few dark blue labels.

REPRODUCTIONS

1436	Dozier Boys	Pretty Eyes (Original unknown on 45 RPM)
1458	Jackie Brenston	Rocket 88
1494	Harmonica Frank	Howlin' Tomcat
1521	Clefs	We Three
1604	Chuck Berry	Maybellene
1614	Five Notes	Show Me The Way
1650	Bobby Sisco	Go Go Go
1653	Chuck Berry	School Day
1662	Billy Barrix	Cool Off Baby
1671	Chuck Berry	Rock & Roll Music

1683	**Chuck Berry**	Sweet Little Sixteen
1691	**Chuck Berry**	Johnny B. Goode
1700	**Chuck Berry**	Carol
1708	**Re Vels**	False Alarm
1722	**Chuck Berry**	Little Queenie
1729	**Chuck Berry**	Memphis Tennessee
1730	**Rusty York**	Sugaree
1822	**Tiny Tip**	Matrimony

CHEX

There are a number of interesting variations of "I Love You" by the Volumes. The first release had the group name misspelled as Valumes and the record as 1000.2. The release with the correct spelling appeared two ways, one with the record number 1002 at the bottom, the other with the number on the right. The latter is much more common. A reissue (not a reproduction) also exists, but the label is more of a white color, and RE 1-71 is in the wax.

REPRODUCTIONS

None.

COED

Different sizes of print were used indiscriminately on portions of the red and black label.

SPECIFICS

500 and 501 — red and black label, COED in red print.

502 thru 533 — red and black label, COED in red and black print.
506 has two totally different pressings, one crediting Coronation Music and a matrix number on the label, the other crediting January Corp., and without the matrix number. The first of these appears with the early style label on the B side.

529 — begins black label.

REPRODUCTIONS

501	Crests	Pretty Little Angel
506	Crests	16 Candles
562	Johnny Maestro	Besame Baby

DECCA

There is a large overlap period with the early Decca label. Number 29124 was pressed on both styles, but since this was a hit, the star label is more likely a later pressing of the same song. Number 29368 was not a hit record and is listed below as the starting point for the label with the star. One Decca pressing plant continued to use the earlier style without the star creating the large amount of overlap. Many, but not all Decca records were machine stamped.

SPECIFICS

48000 R & B series and 28000 thru 30657 — black label with lines at the sides.

29368 thru 31099 — black label with a star in the middle.

31093 — begins black label with multicolor.

REPRODUCTIONS

48241	Skylarks	The Glory Of Love
48319	Mello Tones	I'm Just Another One In Love With You
48323	Barons	My Baby's Gone
28092	Blenders	I'd Be A Fool Again
29293	Barons	Forget About Me
29298	Singing Wanderers	The Wrong Party Again
29603	Tangiers	Tabarin
29854	Buddy Holly	Blue Days Black Nights
29914	Chorals	Rock And Roll Baby
29936	Autry Inman	Be Bop Baby
29940	Johnny Carroll	Rock & Roll Ruby

29941	**Johnny Carroll**	Wild Wild Women
30013	**Johnny Carroll**	Hot Rock
30053	**Al Coker**	Don't Go Baby
30060	**Roy Hall**	Diggin' The Boggie
30166	**Buddy Holly**	Modern Don Juan
30206	**Jackie Lee Cochran**	Ruby Pearl
30277	**Don Woody**	You're Barking Up The Wrong Tree
30350	**Five Secrets**	See You Next Year
30434	**Buddy Holly**	That'll Be The Day
30543	**Buddy Holly**	Love Me
30576	**Hi Fives**	How Can I Win
30650	**Buddy Holly**	Ting A Ling
30654	**Van Dykes**	Run Betty Run
30657	**Hi Fives**	Dorothy
30688	**Fortunes**	How Clever Of You
30722	**5 Shillings**	Letter To An Angel
30762	**Van Dykes**	Come On Baby
30916	**Starfires**	Love Is Here To Stay
30994	**Four Lovers**	Please Take A Chance
31015	**Treble Chords**	Teresa
31312	**Dreamers**	Carole
31382	**Tony Sheridan**	My Bonnie

DEL FI

Even though Del Fi started with record number 4101 the first three releases have been seen only on white promotional copies. Numbers 4104 and 4105 have not been seen in any form and it is not known whether they exist. The remainder of the label is detailed below.

SPECIFICS

4106 thru 4125 — "circles" label.
4110 exists as an all green label variation.

4127 thru 4148 — blue label with sawtooth border.

4148 — begins black label with sawtooth border.

REPRODUCTIONS

4110	**Ritchie Valens**	Donna
4158	**Little Caesar**	Those Oldies But Goodies

DOOTO(NE)

Many Dooto and Dootone releases have been reissued. Any record prior to number 414 should not be on the yellow label and records that came on the maroon label with an address should not have a zip code as part of that address. Multicolor labels are also later pressings. Dooto(ne) also put 45-DOO- in the dead wax of nearly all of their originals.

SPECIFICS

300 thru 413 — primarily Dootone maroon, some black, blue, or red, with or without the address beneath Dootone. A few Dooto.
359 thru 413 — primarily with the address.
359 — Dooto with address is far more common (and less valuable) than Dootone.
407 — Dootone without address.
409 — Dootone with or without address.
412 — Dooto with address.
413 — Dooto with address.

414 thru 438 — yellow and red Dooto.

441 — begins yellow and blue Dooto.

REPRODUCTIONS

345	**Penguins**	No There Ain't No News Today
348	**Penguins**	Earth Angel
353	**Penguins**	Love Will Make Your Mind Go Wild

DOT

The early (1000 - 1289) Dot series ran somewhat concurrently with the later (15000) series and there was some overlap in label styles between the two. Many records have been reissued on the black label but carry a different, low digit, record number.

SPECIFICS

1000 thru 1100 — flat maroon or shiny brown label, gold print.

1101 thru 1150 — yellow label.

1151 thru 1289 — flat maroon, silver print.

15000 thru 15507 — shiny brown (early) or flat maroon.

15501 — begins black label with some maroon label overlap.

REPRODUCTIONS

1043	**Four Dots**	My Dear (Original unknown on 45 RPM.)
1188	**Counts**	Darling Dear
1199	**Counts**	Baby Don't You Know
1204	**Five Dots**	The Other Night
1210	**Counts**	My Dear My Darling
1226	**Counts**	Waitin' Around For You
1235	**Counts**	Let Me Go Lover
1243	**Counts**	Love And Understanding
1265	**Counts**	I Need You Tonight
1275	**Counts**	To Our Love
15114	**Cap-Tans**	With All My Love
15706	**Mickey Gilley**	Call Me Shorty
15766	**Jimmy Newman**	Carry On
15773	**Dick D'Agostin**	Nancy Lynne
16056	**Phantom**	Love Me

DUB

DUB records were produced in two places, California and Arkansas, and this is reflected in the address appearing on the label (California shown). The reproduction of 2840 is extremely good, and if in doubt the Arkansas press is a safe bet because of the machine stamped numbers. Record number 2843 has also been done, but the label is poor and the information on the Arkansas press still applies.

REPRODUCTIONS

2840	**Don Head**	Goin' Strong
2843	**Edsels**	Rama Lama Ding Dong

EMBER

Nearly the entire Ember series has been reissued on the red and black label. This includes records originally released on the later style labels. The reissues do not have Manufactured By Herald Records at the top of the label. The -45 suffix was used extensively in the dead wax.

SPECIFICS

101 — maroon label.

1001 thru 1039 — red and black label, some orange labels.
1001 thru 1024 — many, but not all, used a small record number.
1025 thru 1039 — many, but not all, used a bold record number.

1039 thru 1064 — multicolor label.

1065 — begins black label and a few multicolor.

REPRODUCTIONS

1005	**Five Satins**	In The Still Of The Night
1008	**Five Satins**	Wonderful Girl
1013	**Starlarks**	Fountain Of Love

1014	Five Satins	Oh Happy Day
1019	Five Satins	To The Aisle
1022	Marktones	Hold Me Close
1025	Five Satins	Our Anniversary
1027	Lee Allen	Walkin' With Mr. Lee
1029	Silhouettes	Get A Job
1037	Silhouettes	Bing Bong
1056	Five Satins	Shadows
1061	Five Satins	I'll Be Seeing You
1066	Five Satins	Candlelight
1069	Fabulons	Smoke From Your Cigarette
1070	Five Satins	Wishing Ring
1071	Illusions	Can't We Fall In Love

END

There is a common misconception that the black label End pressings were done only on the east coast and the gray labels of the early numbers were west coast first presses. This positively is not true. In fact, west coast presses on the black label are identifiable by the solid horizontal lines.

SPECIFICS

1000 thru 1010 — black label.

1010 thru 1045 — gray or white label with the dog.

1046 — begins multicolor or white label with the dog.

REPRODUCTIONS

1003	Lewis Lymon	Your Last Chance
1007	Lewis Lymon	I Found Out Why
1011	Tunemasters	I've Lied (black label)
1096	Delsatins	I'll Pray For You

FEE BEE

The Fee Bee series is somewhat confusing because certain records were reissued with a different flip side. This would, in effect, be a first pressing of this particular record but a second press of the reissued side. As described in the specifics below, the two prominent releases, "Come Go With Me" and "Wispering Bells," should have two sets of two equal thickness horizontal lines to be considered first press.

SPECIFICS

201 thru 233 — primarily orange with the bee and two sets of double, equal thickness, horizontal lines (see photo). Numbers 206 and 221 were originally issued without the bee.

REPRODUCTIONS

205	**Dell Vikings**	Come Go With Me B/W Whispering Bells

FLIP

There is a common misconception that parenthesis around the matrix number on the Flip label is an indication of a reissue. Originals, even on the maroon label, may or may not have the parenthesis. There is no apparent pattern to their use. A somewhat smaller record number was used later in the series, and earlier (prior to 327) issues having this smaller number may be less desirable even though they are also 50's pressings. The prefix 45-FL in the wax, and delta pressings, appear on nearly all Flip releases. Do not confuse this label with the southern Flip label that had 500 series releases.

SPECIFICS

301 thru 304 — maroon label.

304 thru 320 — blue label with horizontal lines.

321 thru 324 — blue label without horizontal lines.

325 thru 364 — blue label with horizontal lines.

REPRODUCTIONS

305	**Flippers**	You Yakity Yak Too Much
312	**Vel Aires**	Heaven In My Arms
315	**Sixteens**	A Casual Look
323	**King Bees**	Give Me Your Number
330	**Arthur Lee Maye**	Cause You're Mine Alone

GEE

SPECIFICS

1 thru 12 — yellow and green label.

1000 thru 1052 — red and black label.
1000 thru 1021 and 1026 thru 1039 had 45 RPM on both sides of the label.
1022 thru 1025 and 1039 thru 1052 had Trade Mark on the left and Reg. U.S. Pat. Off. on the right of the label. Note 1039 came both ways.

1053 — begins gray label.

REPRODUCTIONS

10	**Coins**	Blue Can't Get No Place With You (only a few known 45's)
11	**Coins**	S.R. Blues
12	**Colonials**	Two Loves Have I
1004	**Valtones**	You Belong To My Heart
1005	**Emanons**	Change Of Time
1009	**Quintones**	I'm Willing
1020	**Jets**	Heaven Above Me
1029	**Carol Blades**	When Will I Know

GONE

The first three records on the Gone label, 5001 thru 5003, were black with shadow print. 5004 thru 5056 were also on a black label, but without the shadow print. A minor variation in this label, double horizontal lines versus single horizontal lines, is merely a west coast pressing as opposed to an east coast pressing. Even though the multicolored label began with number 5057 the black label was used well into this series.

SPECIFICS

5001 thru 5003 — black label with block shadow print.

5004 thru 5056 — black label with clown.

5057 — begins multicolor label with clown.
Records were pressed well into this series on the earlier black label.

REPRODUCTIONS

5013	**Kings**	Don't Go
5015	**Willows**	Let's Fall In Love

GORDY

Many Gordy releases have been reissued on label styles similar to the originals. There are two things to keep in mind in addition to the specifics listed below. First, the copyright symbol and date did not appear on the label prior to record number 7032. This date, when it did appear, corresponds closely to the release date of the record. Later dates, or dates on records that did not originally have them, are good indications of a reissue. Second, the shade of purple on reissues of the early style label is somewhat lighter than the originals.

HULL

SPECIFICS

711 thru 712 — pink label.

713 thru 715 — black label without ring.

716 thru 721 — red or black label wlth ring.

722 thru 742 — red label without ring.

743 — begins tan or red label.

REPRODUCTIONS

712	Mabel Lee	Dearest Dream
713	Heartbeats	Darling How Long
716	Heartbeats	People Are Talking
717	Avons	Our Love Will Never End
721	Beltones	I Talk To My Echo
722	Avons	Baby
723	Sparks	Danny Boy
725	Joan & Joy	You're My Prescription
726	Avons	You Are So Close To Me
727	Legends	The Legend Of Love
728	Avons	Please Come Back To Me
730	Desires	Let It Please Be You
731	Avons	What Love Can Do
732	Elegants	Little Boy Blue
733	Desires	Set Me Free
735	Monotones	Reading The Book Of Love
740	Limelites	Daddy's Home
751	Limelites	What Did Daddy Do?
757	Limelites	Stick By Me

IMPERIAL

SPECIFICS

5180 thru 5290 — blue script label.

5291 thru 5357 — red script label.

5357 thru 5553 — primarily red block print, some early blue block print. Note the overlap with the black label. Some issues in this series were also on a maroon label.

5461 — begins black label.

REPRODUCTIONS

5058	**Fats Domino**	The Fat Man (Original unknown on 45 RPM)
5067	**Smiley Lewis**	Tee Nah Nah (Original unknown on 45 RPM)
5072	**Smiley Lewis**	Growing Old (Original unknown on 45 RPM)
5145	**Fats Domino**	Careless Love (Original unknown on 45 RPM)
5167	**Fats Domino**	You Know I Miss You
5197	**Fats Domino**	Trust In Me
5211	**Fat Man Matthews**	When Boy Meets Girl
5236	**Bobby Mitchell**	Rock Em Back
5250	**Bobby Mitchell**	One Friday Morning
5254	**Love Notes**	Surrender Your Heart
5266	**Hawks**	Candy Girl
5268	**Smiley Lewis**	Down The Road
5272	**Fats Domino**	Little School Girl
5292	**Hawks**	It Ain't That Way
5295	**Bobby Mitchell**	Meant For Me
5296	**Smiley Lewis**	Can't Stop Loving You
5307	**Pelicans**	Chimes
5309	**Bobby Mitchell**	She Couldn't Be Found
5320	**Bees**	I Want To Be Loved

5335	Kidds	Are You Forgetting Me
5348	Fats Domino	Ain't It A Shame
5349	Smiley Lewis	Real Gone Lover
5386	Fats Domino	I'm In Love again
5396	Fats Domino	When My Dreamboat Comes Home
5401	Dukes	Teardrop Eyes
5407	Fats Domino	Blueberry Hill
5417	Fats Domino	Blue Monday
5422	Roy Brown	Saturday Night
5428	Fats Domino	I'm Walkin'
5451	Weldon Rogers	So Long Good Luck And Goodbye
5482	Dennis Herrold	Hip Hip Baby
5528	Ricky Nelson	Poor Little Fool
5606	Fats Domino	I'm Gonna Be A Wheel Someday
5675	Fats Domino	Walkin' To New Orleans
5704	Fats Domino	My Girl Josephine
5741	Ricky Nelson	Travelin' Man

JAMIE

SPECIFICS

1000 thru 1101 — black or pink label.

1101 thru 1109 — yellow label, block print without Hollywood.

1111 thru 1124 — yellow label, design at top with Hollywood.

1125 — begins yellow and white label.

REPRODUCTIONS

None.

JERDEN

One reproduction is available on Jerden, "Louie Louie" by the Kingsmen. The reproduction is easily distinguished by the 340 in the dead wax.

REPRODUCTIONS

712	Kingsmen	Louie Louie

JOSIE

SPECIFICS

760 thru 829 — tan label with JOZ, brown print.

830 thru 845 — tan label with JOZ, red print.
835 exists on the earlier brown print label.

846 — begins tan label with JOSIE.
846 exists on the earlier brown print label.

REPRODUCTIONS

760	Starlings	My Plea For Love
762	Four Bars	Grief By Day Grief By Night
771	Teardrops	My Heart
779	Qualitones	Roxanna
795	Limelighters	Cabin Hideaway
823	Blue Notes	Wagon Wheels
891	Chaperones	Man From The Moon
900	Vidaltones	Forever
920	Styles	I Love You For Sentimental Reasons

JUBILEE

SPECIFICS

5000 thru 5092 — blue label without line under JUBILEE.

5093 thru 5340 — blue label, line under JUBILEE.

5338 — begins black label.

REPRODUCTIONS

5001	Orioles	Dare To Dream (Original unknown on 45 RPM)
5002	Orioles	It Seems So Long Ago (Original unknown on 45 RPM)
5008	Orioles	I Challenge Your Kiss (Original unknown on 45 RPM)
5009	Orioles	A Kiss And A Rose (Original unknown on 45 RPM)
5016	Orioles	Forgive And Forget
5018	Orioles	Is My Heart Wasting Time (Original unknown on 45 RPM)
5025	Orioles	At Night
5026	Orioles	Moonlight (Original unknown on 45 RPM)
5028	Orioles	You're Gone (Original unknown on 45 RPM)
5031	Orioles	We're Supposed To Be Through (Original unknown on 45 RPM)
5037	Orioles	I Need You So (Original unknown on 45 RPM)
5040	Orioles	I Cross My Fingers
5051	Orioles	I Miss You So

5054	Sultans	Lemon Squeezing Daddy (Original unknown on 45 RPM)
5055	Orioles	Pal Of Mine (Original unknown on 45 RPM)
5057	Orioles	Would I Love You (Original unknown on 45 RPM)
5061	Orioles	I'm Just A Fool In Love
5065	Orioles	Baby Please Don't Go
5071	Orioles	When You're Not Around
5074	Orioles	Trust In Me
5077	Sultans	Blues At Dawn
5079	Marylanders	I'm A Sentimental Fool
5082	Orioles	It's Over Because We're Through
5091	Marylanders	Make Me Thrill Again
5092	Orioles	Don't Cry Baby
5102	Orioles	You Belong To Me
5104	Five Sharps	Stormy Weather (Original unknown on 45 RPM)
5108	Orioles	Teardrops On My Pillow
5115	Orioles	Dem Days
5120	Orioles	I Cover The Waterfront

KING

King had two series of records running concurrently. One, primarily on a maroon label, ran from 500 thru 1512. The other began with number 4100 and was on a variety of blue labels. Many of these records were on 78 RPM issues in the forties. The information listed below begins around 1952, and covers all known reproductions. The prefix K-45- appears in the dead wax of most original 45's.

SPECIFICS

1280 thru 1470 — maroon label.

1470 thru 1512 — blue label.

4466 thru **4544** — blue label with AA after the number.

4545 thru **4834** — blue label, no AA.

4835 thru **5266** — blue label, small High Fidelity.

5267 — begins blue label, larger (1/8") High Fidelity.

REPRODUCTIONS

4466	Swallows	Since You've Been Away (Original unknown on 45 RPM)
4485	Wynonie Harris	Lovin' Machine
4497	Tiny Bradshaw	Knockin' Blues
4501	Swallows	Eternally
4515	Swallows	Tell Me Why
4525	Swallows	You Left Me
4533	Swallows	I Only Have Eyes For You
4558	Checkers	Flame In My Heart
4581	Checkers	Night's Curtains
4596	Checkers	My Prayer Tonight
4612	Swallows	Laugh
4626	Checkers	Ghost Of My Baby
4632	Swallows	Nobody's Lovin' Me
4656	Swallows	Trust Me
4663	Orchids	I've Been A Fool From The Start
4665	Magic Tones	When I Kneel Down To Pray
4670	Ink Spots	Here In My Lonely Room
4676	Swallows	I'll Be Waiting
4681	Magic Tones	How Can You Treat Me This Way
4697	Strangers	My Friend
4761	Roy Brown	Fannie Brown Got Married
4772	Admirals	Left With A Broken Heart
4778	Five Wings	Johnny Is Gone
4781	Five Wings	Teardrops Are Falling
4821	Strangers	Without A Friend
4898	Hurricanes	Raining In My Heart
4926	Hurricanes	Your Promise To Me

4927	Mac Curtis	If I Had Me A Woman
4935	Little Willie John	Fever
4940	Bill Beach	Peg Pants
4947	Hurricanes	Dear Mother
4949	Mac Curtis	Grandaddy's Rockin'
4950	Bill Doggett	Honky Tonk
4971	Charlie Feathers	Everybody's Loving My Baby
4995	Mac Curtis	That Ain't Nothin'
4997	Charlie Feathers	One Hand Loose
5018	Hurricanes	Fallen Angel
5022	Charlie Feathers	Nobody's Woman
5043	Charlie Feathers	Too Much Alike
5116	Cecil McNabb	Clock Tickin' Rhythm
5119	Fascinators	Tee Vee
5158	Van Dykes	The Bells Are Ringing
5236	Hank Mizell	Jungle Rock
5251	Five Keys	I Took Your Love For A Toy
5341	Hank Ballard	Finger Poppin' Time
5365	Ronnie Mollern	Fat Mama
5377	Mascots	The Story Of My Heart
5400	Hank Ballard	Let's Go Let's Go
5435	Mascots	Lonely Rain
5633	Interludes	Darling I'll Be True
5766	Tony Dell	My Girl
5799	Little Willie John	Talk To Me
5999	James Brown	Papa's Got A Brand New Bag

LEGRAND

Legrand has two styles of reissues that are close to the originals in appearance. One is similar to the purple label but is reddish in color. The other is like the later gold, red and white label except the white is missing.

SPECIFICS

1001 thru 1005 — purple label.

1005 — begins gold, red and white label.

REPRODUCTIONS

1003	Gary Bonds	New Orleans
1008	Gary Bonds	Quarter To Three
1009	Gary Bonds	School Is Out

MGM

SPECIFICS

55000 series — yellow label.

10000 thru 12841 — yellow label.

12826 — begins black label. Note overlap.

REPRODUCTIONS

55004	Hide A Ways	Cherie
55011	Twilighters	Little Did I Dream
55014	Twilighters	Half Angel
11428	Crickets	You're Mine
11507	Crickets	For You I Have Eyes
11850	Ramblers	Vadunt Un Va Da Song
12240	Marvin Rainwater	Hot And Cold
12263	Andy Starr	Rockin' Rollin' Stone
12284	Buck Griffin	Stutterin' Papa
12315	Andy Starr	She's A Going Jessie
12338	Notes	Trust In Me
12364	Andy Starr	Round And Round
12421	Andy Starr	One More Time
12422	Ron Hargrove	Latch On
12482	Cecil Campbell	Rock And Roll Fever
12588	Connie Francis	Who's Sorry Now
12677	Conway Twitty	It's Only Make Believe
12793	Connie Francis	Lipstick On Your Collar
13051	Connie Francis	Baby's First Christmas
13213	Beatles	My Bonnie

MERCURY

SPECIFICS

5000 and 8000 series — maroon label.

70001 thru 71080 — maroon or black label, also pink (R&B) or green (country) labels.

71040 — begins maroon or black with Mercury in an oval.

REPRODUCTIONS

5764	Ravens	There's No Use Pretending
5800	Ravens	Begin The Beguine
5870	Wini Brown	Your Happiness Is Mine
8270	Wini Brown	Be Anything Be Mine
70019	Dreamers	Please Don't Leave Me
70060	Ravens	Don't Mention My Name
70119	Ravens	Come A Little Bit Closer
70143	4 Plaid Throats	My Inspiration
70213	Ravens	Who'll Be The Fool
70240	Ravens	Without A Song
70307	Ravens	September Song
70330	Jimmy Ricks	Going Home
70413	Ravens	Love Is No Dream
70558	Griffins	I Swear By All The Stars Above
70610	Penguins	Be Mine Or Be A Fool
70633	Platters	Only You
70650	Griffins	Scheming
70654	Penguins	It Only Happens With You
70679	Cashmeres	There's A Rumor
70698	Red Prysock	Hand Clapin'
70703	Penguins	Devil That I See
70753	Platters	Great Pretender
70762	Penguins	A Christmas Prayer
70770	Roy Moss	You're My Big Baby Now
70799	Penguins	My Troubles Are Not At An End

70826	Eddie Bond	Rockin' Daddy
70852	George & Earl	Done Gone
70858	Roy Moss	You Don't Know My Mind
70882	Eddie Bond	Slip Slip Slipin' In
70893	Platters	My Prayer
70941	Eddie Bond	Boppin' Bonnie
70943	Penguins	Earth Angel
71033	Penguins	Will You Be Mine
71150	Five Dreams	Up All Night Long
71155	Little Beats	Someone For Me
71179	Sleepy La Beef	All The Time
71209	Jimmy Edwards	Love Bug Crawl
71239	Ivories	Me & You
71289	Platters	Twilight Time
71293	Miller Bros.	If I Had A Car
71309	Medallionaires	Magic Moonlight
71343	Big Bopper	Chantilly Lace
71383	Platters	Smoke Gets In Your Eyes
71434	Eastmen	Lover Come Home
71437	Derbys	Night After Night
71516	Jimmy McCracklin	Georgia Slop
71612	Ben Hewitt	Whirlwind Blues
71723	Buddy & Ella Johnson	I Don't Want Nobody

MILESTONE

Dark blue labels are second pressings on Milestone.

SPECIFICS

2001 — maroon label, Milestone written straight across.

2003 — maroon or shiny red label with Milestone written in an arc.

2004 thru 2006 — pink label with milestone marker at the top.

2007 — begins turquoise and white or all turquoise with milestone marker at the top.

REPRODUCTIONS

2003	Paradons	Diamonds And Pearls

MODERN

Many of the early Modern releases were 78 RPM only. Nearly all of the 45 RPM releases had the prefix 45-MM- before the number in the dead wax.

SPECIFICS

826 thru 980 — primarily shiny red, also blue or black.

980 — begins primarily flat black, a few blue or maroon.

REPRODUCTIONS

807	Robbins	Rockin' (Original unknown on 45 RPM)
933	Marvin & Johnny	Cherry Pie
939	Native Boys	Native Girl
944	Crowns	Set My Heart Free
964	Cobras	Sindy
971	Cadets	If It Is Wrong
994	Cadets	Stranded In The Jungle
1002	Young Jessie	Hit Git And Split

MOTOWN

Motown has a situation similar to Gordy where early releases have been reissued on the same label style. The same logic applies with regard to the copyright symbol and date. This symbol and date did not appear on the label prior to record number 1057, and also corresponded closely to the release of the record.

SPECIFICS

1/2 and 1000 thru 1011 — pink label.

1011 — begins blue label.

REPRODUCTIONS

Many of the Motown reproductions have drill holes through the label.

1056	Mary Wells	My Guy
1060	Supremes	Where Did Our Love Go
1062	Four Tops	Baby I Need Your Loving
1066	Supremes	Baby Love
1068	Supremes	Come See About Me
1073	Four Tops	Ask The Lonely
1074	Supremes	Stop In The Name Of Love
1076	Four Tops	I Can't Help Myself
1163	Jackson 5	ABC
1177	Jackson 5	Mama's Pearl

OKEH

Originals on the Okeh label are easily distinguished from the reproductions because the information in the dead wax is machine stamped.

SPECIFICS

6800 thru 7092 — purple label with Okeh ½" high.

7093 thru 7147 — purple or yellow label with Okeh ½" high.

7141 thru 7209 — purple label with Okeh ¾" high.

7209 — begins purple label with Okeh in white.

REPRODUCTIONS

6820	Mr. Google Eyes	Rough And Rocky Road
6825	Ravens	Wiffenpoof Song
6832	Royals	Dreams Of You
6843	Ravens	Everything But You

6888	Ravens	Mam'selle
6900	5 Blue Flames	Blue Boy
7046	Hi Lites	I Found A Love
7076	Schoolboys	Please Say You Want Me
7095	Billy Stewart	Baby You're My Only Love

OLD TOWN

Old Town had two label styles near the end of their series. A black and blue label was used at the same time as the pale blue label, and both are considered original for number 1130. The pale blue label, however, is the only first pressing for number 1094.

SPECIFICS

300 thru 305 — black label, same design as 1029.

790 thru 793 — yellow label with green print.

1000 thru 1012 — yellow label with Old English print.

1013 thru 1028 — yellow label with horizontal ropes, open face print.

1029 thru 1051 — yellow label with open face print, no ropes.

1052 — begins primarily pale blue, blue and black label used later.

REPRODUCTIONS

790	5 Crowns	You Could Be My Love
792	5 Crowns	Lullaby Of The Bells (Original unknown on 45 RPM)
1000	Solitaires	Blue Valentine
1003	Co-Eds	I'm In Love
1006	Solitaires	Please Remember My Heart
1008	Solitaires	Lonely
1009	Valentines	Tonight Kathleen
1010	Solitaires	I Don't Stand A Ghost Of A Chance

1011	Cleftones	My Dearest Darling
1012	Solitaires	My Dear
1015	Solitaires	Magic Rose
1024	Supremes	Tonight
1026	Solitaires	The Angels Sang
1027	Coeds	Love You Baby All The Time
1028	Royaltones	Latin Love
1030	Ruth McFadden	School Boy
1032	Solitaires	Nothing Like A Little Love
1034	Solitaires	Walkin' Along
1042	Fi Tones	My Faith
1044	Solitaires	Thrill Of Love
1047	Robert & Johnny	We Belong Together
1049	Solitaires	Walkin' And Talkin'
1053	Inspirators	Starlight Tonight
1062	Fiestas	So Fine
1094	Capris	There's A Moon Out Tonight
1130	Earls	Remember Then
1194	Bobby & Betty Lou	Sugar (DJ)

ORIGINAL SOUND

SPECIFICS

1 thru 14 — black label with the print straight across, slight variations in thickness and composition of print.

17 — begins black or gray label with the print in an arc. Initially a red border was used on a black label, but this was dropped mid-way through the series and the remainder were on a plain black or gray label.

REPRODUCTIONS

None.

PHILLES

Records numbered 100 thru 108 were issued on the orange label, although 106 thru 108 are rarely seen this way, and most collectors are satisfied with the blue label. Changes etc., are detailed below.

SPECIFICS

100 thru 104 — orange label.

105 and 106 — orange label, or blue label with an address at the bottom.
106 most commonly appears on the blue label but should still have the address at the bottom.

107 and 108 — orange label, or blue label without address. Both commonly appear on blue without the address.

109 thru 115 — blue label, no address.
109X exists, the only difference is the B side titling.

116 — begins yellow label.
114 and 115 were also pressed on the yellow label.
119X exists, and is a completely different recording than 119.

REPRODUCTIONS

100	**Crystals**	There's No Other
102	**Crystals**	Uptown
106	**Crystals**	He's A Rebel (blue label)
111	**Crystals**	Do The Screw
112	**Crystals**	Da Do Ron Ron
115	**Crystals**	Then He Kissed Me (blue label)
116	**Ronettes**	Be My Baby
118	**Ronettes**	Baby I Love You
121	**Ronettes**	Do I Love You
123	**Ronettes**	Walking In The Rain
124	**Righteous Bros.**	You've Lost That Lovin' Feeling
129	**Righteous Bros.**	Unchained Melody
131	**Ike & Tina**	River Deep Mountain High

PROMO

The Promo label is included because of the second press of "A Million To One" by Jimmy Charles. The first press should look like the one in the photo section. The second press is distinguished by the much larger print. Although Promo also had a multicolor label there seems to be very little issued that would be of collector interest.

REPRODUCTIONS

None.

RAMA

SPECIFICS

1 thru 196 — blue label.
The original of number 3 has solid horizontal lines as opposed to the normal double horizontal lines.

197 thru 222 — red label with 45 RPM on both sides.

221 — begins red label with Reg. U.S. Pat. Off. on the left, 45 RPM on the right.

REPRODUCTIONS

1	**Five Budds**	I Was A Fool
2	**Five Budds**	I Want Her Back
3	**Crows**	Seven Lonely Days
10	**Crows**	Heartbreaker
21	**Buccaneers**	The Stars Will Remember
24	**Buccaneers**	You Did Me Wrong
29	**Crows**	Untrue
30	**Crows**	Miss You
50	**Crows**	Baby Doll
110	**Wrens**	Eleven Roses
166	**Bells**	What Can I Tell Her Now
174	**Wrens**	Serenade Of The Bells

184	Wrens	I Wont Come To Your Wedding
194	Wrens	C'est La Vie
198	Pretenders	I've Got To Have You Baby
201	Valentines	Twenty Minutes
209	Rainbows	Minnie
210	Pretenders	Lover
226	Roc LaRue	Teenage Blues

RCA

All of the RCA records that are within the scope of this book are primarily on a black label with a dog at the top and most are machine stamped in the wax. A variation worth noting is the addition of a pair of horizontal silver lines that were added to some releases. These are merely variations, and definitely not DJ copies, they are also usually worth a little more than their counterparts without the lines. The first three reproductions listed below were released in 1951 on the blue/green label that preceded the black label. This label is not to be confused with the green label used for country records. The record number on the country label was prefixed with the number 48. The releases described in this book were prefixed with the number 47. The early grey label carried a 50 prefix.

REPRODUCTIONS

4327	Heartbreakers	Heartbreaker
4483	Billy Bunn & Buddies	I Need A Shoulder To Cry On (DJ)
4508	Heartbreakers	You're So Necessary To Me
4657	Billy Bunn & Buddies	That's When Your Heartaches Begin (DJ)
4662	Heartbreakers	Why Don't I
4849	Heartbreakers	There Is Time
5175	Robins	My Heart's The Biggest Fool
5271	Robins	Oh Why
5434	Robins	How Would You Know
5564	Robins	Don't Stop Now (DJ)
7853	Sam Cooke	That's It—I Quit—I'm Movin' On

RIBBON

Reissues exist on the earlier red ribbon label. The print used for the title is larger than what was used for the first pressings. First pressing is shown.

SPECIFICS

6901 thru 6905 — red label, also orange on 6901.

6904 — begins black and red label.

REPRODUCTIONS

None.

ROULETTE

Roulette's initial series is somewhat confusing because of the variety in label styles. Many opinions exist on which was the absolute first press, but all styles seem equally desirable. The green label 7000 series was used for country western records.

SPECIFICS

4001 thru 4005 — red label with half wheel, red or maroon label with the full wheel, orange label delta pressing. 4001 and 4002 were also pressed on the plain red label.

4006 thru 4008 — not known to exist.

4009 thru 4045 — plain red label, orange label delta pressing.
4010 exists as the earlier half wheel on a delta pressing.
4015, 4018, 4031, and 4045 had additional pressings by Capitol distinguished by their machine stamp in the wax.
4018 has some pressings with "From The Warner Bros. Motion Pict. Jamboree"
4031 early pressings credit Evans-Hughes-Rodgers as writers, Favorite Music as publishers. Later pressings show Campbell-Newman as writers, Folkways as publishers.
4045 exists on the white label with stripes.

4048 thru 4432 — white label with stripes.

4048 thru 4108 have a black circle above the record number without the eight point star inside, 4109 has the star, 4110 thru 4114 do not, 4115 has the star, 4116 thru 4119 do not, 4120 on have the star.

4154 early pressings credit Ron Hawkins-Jacqueline Magill as writers, Patricia Music as publishers, and the artist as Ronnie Hawkins. Later pressings have Chuck Berry as the writer and Art Music (should be Arc) as the publishers with Ronnie Hawkins and The Hawks as artists.

4438 thru 4515 — dark pink, earlier white label as a delta pressing.

4515 thru 4762 — orange/yellow without gray circle.

4775 — begins orange/yellow with gray circle.

REPRODUCTIONS

4549	**Chances**	Through A Long And Sleepless Night
4580	**Devotions**	Snow White
7001	**Jimmy Lloyd**	The Beginning Of The End

RPM

RPM is the sister label of Modern and used the same prefix in most of their 45 RPM releases, 45-MM- appears in the dead wax before the matrix number. Many early releases were 78 RPM only.

SPECIFICS

339 thru 360 — black, blue, maroon or red label, script print.

361 thru 460 — red or blue label, block style print.

453 — begins flat black label. Note overlap.

REPRODUCTIONS

316	**Nic Nacs**	You Didn't Want My Love (Original unknown on 45 RPM)

399	Meadow Larks	Love Only You
406	Meadow Larks	LFMST Blues (Original unknown on 45 RPM)
424	Crowns	Truly
429	Crowns	Love Me Always
438	Crowns	Please Don't Leave Me
446	Trojans	As Long As I Have You
499	Paul Anka	I Confess
502	Don Cole	Snake Eyed Mama

RUST

The Rust label is included because of the large number of reissues. As noted below, nearly every original issued was on a white label.

SPECIFICS

5022 thru 5130 — primarily white label, a few blue label southern presses.

REPRODUCTIONS

None.

SAVOY

Numbers 1000 thru 1099 and 1200 thru 1499 were not released by Savoy. The majority of releases in the 900 series were jazz/pop music, but some R&B records have appeared using these numbers. These are not legitimate releases. Most Savoy records have at least part of a number machine stamped in the dead wax. Exceptions to this start appearing around mid 1500.

SPECIFICS

731 thru 899 — maroon label.
726, 738, 752, and 762 are not known to exist on 45 RPM.

PHOTO SECTION

ACE-white • ACE-yellow • ALADDIN-blue
ALADDIN-maroon • ALADDIN-black • AMP3
APT-multicolor • APT-black • ARGO-ship
ARGO-black • ARGO-tan • ATCO-maroon

ATCO-yellow • ATLANTIC-yellow • ATLANTIC-red no fan
ATLANTIC-red w/fan • AUDICON-red • AUDICON-multicolor
BACK BEAT-white • BACK BEAT-red • BRUNSWICK-maroon
BRUNSWICK-orange • BRUNSWICK-black • CAMEO-orange

CAMEO-red/black • CAPITOL-large logo • CAPITOL-small logo
CAPITOL-logo on the left • CAPITOL-swirl • CHALLENGE-blue
CHALLENGE-arc • CHALLENGE-maroon • CHALLENGE-green/blue
CHALLENGE-black • CHANCELLOR-pink • CHANCELLOR-black

CHECKER-web • CHECKER-maroon • CHECKER-checkers
CHESS-silver top • CHESS-blue • CHESS-multicolor
CHESS-black • CHEX • COED-red print
COED-red and black print • COED-black • DECCA-lines at sides

DECCA-star • DECCA-multicolor • DELFI-circles
DELFI-green • DELFI-sawtooth border • DOOTONE-blue
DOOTONE-maroon w/address • DOOTO-yellow • DOT-shiny brown
DOT-maroon • DOT-black • DUB-California

EMBER-red • EMBER-multicolor • EMBER-black
END-black • END-white • END-multicolor
FALCON • FEEBEE • FLIP-maroon
FLIP-blue • GEE-yellow • GEE-without Reg. U.S. Pat. Off.

GEE-with Reg. U.S. Pat. Off. • GEE-gray • GONE-shadow
GONE-black w/clown • GONE-multicolor • GORDY-script
GORDY-arrowhead • HERALD-yellow no flag • HERALD-flag and script
HERALD-multicolor • HERALD-flag and block print • HULL-light pink

HULL-black without ring • HULL-red w/ring • HULL-red no ring
HULL-tan • IMPERIAL-blue script • IMPERIAL-red script
IMPERIAL-red block • IMPERIAL-black • JAMIE-pink
JAMIE-black • JAMIE-without Hollywood • JAMIE-with Hollywood

JAMIE-yellow and white • JERDEN • JOSIE-tan print
JOSIE-red print • JOSIE-multicolor • JUBILEE-no line
JUBILEE-with line • JUBILEE-black • KING-maroon
KING-plain blue • KING-small print • KING-large print

LEGRAND-purple • LEGRAND-gold • MGM-yellow
MGM-black • MERCURY-square • MERCURY-oval
MILESTONE-maroon arc • MILESTONE turquoise • MODERN-red
MODERN-black • MOTOWN-pink • MOTOWN-blue

OKEH-small print • OKEH-yellow • OKEH-large print
OLD TOWN green print • OLD TOWN Old English print • OLD TOWN-ropes
OLD TOWN-no ropes • OLD TOWN-blue • OLD TOWN-blue and black
ORIGINAL SOUND-straight print • ORIGINAL SOUND-arc • PHILLES-orange

PHILLES-blue • PHILLES-yellow • PROMO
RAMA-blue • RAMA-red 45 RPM both sides • RCA-silverline
RIBBON-red • RIBBON-black • ROULETTE-maroon
ROULETTE-half wheel • ROULETTE-plain red • ROULETTE-white

ROULETTE-pink • ROULETTE-orange • RPM-script
RPM-black, block print • RUST • SAVOY-maroon
SAVOY-blue • SHAD-pink • SHAD-blue and white
SINGULAR-blue • SNAP • SPARK-silver top

SPARK-red • SPARK-yellow • SPECIALTY-yellow line
SPECIALTY-without line • SUN • SWAN-white without DON'T DROP OUT
SWAN-black with DON'T DROP OUT • TAMLA-vertical print • TAMLA-globe
TAMLA-yellow and brown • TIARA • TOLLIE-box

TROMMERS-orange • VALMOR-red • VALMOR-black
VEE JAY-thin ring • VEE JAY-thick ring • VEE JAY-rainbow
VEE JAY-plain • VEE JAY-brackets • VEE JAY-oval
WINLEY-3/16 print • WINLEY-1/4 print • WINLEY-with address

ACE RECORDS
YOU AIM TO PLEASE
JIMMY CLANTON
ACE RECORDS
HIGHWAY BOUND
JIMMY CLANTON
Aladdin
BEVERLY HILLS, CALIFORNIA
45-3326
COME ON AND WALK WITH ME
ED TOWNSEND
Aladdin
BEVERLY HILLS, CALIFORNIA
Aladdin
BEVERLY HILLS, CALIFORNIA
45-3413
THE SCRUNCH
LYNN HOPE
DISTRIBUTED BY MERCURY RECORD CORP.
ONE SUMMER NIGHT
THE DANLEERS
APT
45-25005
LITTLE STAR
THE ELEGANTS
A PRODUCT OF AM-PAR RECORD CORP.
APT
A PRODUCT OF AM-PAR RECORD CORP.
45-25005
LITTLE STAR
THE ELEGANTS
Argo
RECORD CORP.
AIN'T GOT NO HOME
CLARENCEHENEY
"FROG MAN"
5259
BEEN SO LONG
(Pastels)
ARGO
THE PASTELS
5287
AUDIO ODYSSEY
EVERYDAY OF THE WEEK
ARGO
THE STUDENTS
5386
45 RPM
ATCO
RECORDS
45-6064
DOWN IN MEXICO
THE COASTERS

45 RPM
ATCO
RECORDS
45-6287
SPEEDO'S BACK IN TOWN
THE COASTERS
ATLANTIC
45 R.P.M.
45-1054
THE DOOR IS STILL OPEN
THE CARDINALS
ATLANTIC
45 R.P.M.
ATLANTIC
45 R.P.M.
UP ON THE ROOF
AUDICON
JUST TO BE WITH YOU
THE PASSIONS
AUDICON
BEAUTIFUL DREAMER
THE PASSIONS
BACK BEAT
RECORDS
45 RPM
SO TOUGH
THE CASUALS
BACK BEAT
DARLING COME TALK TO ME
JOE HINTON
Brunswick
9-55024
REET PETITE
JACKIE WILSON
Brunswick
BABY WORKOUT
JACKIE WILSON
HAVE YOU SEEN HER
Brunswick
CHI-LITES
CAMEO
BUTTERFLY
CHARLIE GRACIE

THE ORLONS
CAMEO
SOUTH STREET
Capitol
THE FIVE KEYS
Capitol
THE FOUR PREPS
MEAN, MEAN MAN
Capitol
4469
WANDA JACKSON
CAN'T BUY ME LOVE
Capitol
5150
THE BEATLES
CHALLENGE
CH-1007-45
FAITH
COMMODORES
CHALLENGE
6920 SUNSET BLVD.
HOLLYWOOD 28, CALIF.
CH-1008-45
WHO'S GONNA CRY
DAVE BURGESS
Challenge
ULTRA HIGH FIDELITY
45 RPM
45 RPM
EL RANCHO ROCK
THE CHAMPS
Challenge
ULTRA HIGH FIDELITY
45 RPM
45 RPM
WARNER BROS RECORDS
HEART AND SOUL
JAN AND DEAN
CHALLENGE
LIES
THE KNICKERBOCKERS
CHANCELLOR
FULL FIDELITY
45 R.P.M.
DEDE DINAH
FRANKIE AVALON
Chancellor
FULL FIDELITY
PARTY LIGHTS
CLAUDINE CLARK

Checker
RECORD CO.
DALE HAWKINS
SAY MAN
CHECKER
BO DIDDLEY
CHECKER
LOVER COME BACK TO ME
THE FLAMINGOS
1084
CHESS
"SCHOOL DAY"
CHUCK BERRY
ROCK & ROLL MUSIC
CHESS
CHUCK BERRY
1671
FAT BOY
CHESS
BILLY STEWART
1820
CHESS
FALSE ALARM
THE RE-VELS
CHEX
Records
45 RPM
1002
DREAMS
THE VOLUMES
COED
PRETTY LITTLE ANGEL
COED
16 CANDLES
COED
CO 569
YOU BELONG TO ME
THE DUPREES
DECCA
UNBREAKABLE
45 RPM
RECORD
ROCK AROUND THE CLOCK
BILL HALEY

DECCA
9-30642
WHEN
KALIN TWINS
MAGIC BUS
DECCA
32362
THE WHO
DEL-FI
new DELPHONIC fidelity
FRAMED
RITCHIE VALENS
4106
Del-Fi
new DELPHONIC fidelity
1058-138
LA BAMBA
RITCHIE VALENS
4110
DEL-FI
4158
THOSE OLDIES BUT GOODIES
LITTLE CAESAR
DOOTONE
348-A-45
HEY SENORITA
THE PENGUINS
DOOTONE
RECORDS
375-A-45
YOU'RE HEAVENLY
THE SAIGONS
1757
dooto
RECORDS
MIX UP
Dot
COQUETTE
KING PERRY
Dot
REG. U. S. PAT. OFFICE
45-15507
CONFIDENTIAL
SONNY KNIGHT
ULTRA HIGH FIDELITY
Dot
45-15781
SUSIE DARLIN'
ROBIN LUKE
DUB

ember
45 RPM
45 RPM
IN THE STILL OF THE NITE
THE FIVE SATINS

EMBER
45RPM
TRY MY LOVE
THE FASHIONS
E-1084

THE FIVE SATINS
EMBER
HIGH FIDELITY
45 RPM
WISHING RING
E-1070

END
End Recording Corp., New York City
45 RPM
45 RPM
E-1001
Vocal
HE'S GONE
THE CHANTELS

end
45 RPM
E-1027
45 RPM
TWO PEOPLE IN THE WORLD
LITTLE ANTHONY AND
THE IMPERIALS

end
45 RPM
45 RPM
Vocal
TRAVELING STRANGER
LITTLE ANTHONY
& THE IMPERIALS

Falcon
FOR YOUR PRECIOUS LOVE
(Brooks & Butler)
JERRY BUTLER
and The Impressions
Falcon 1013

FEE BEE
45 RPM
45 RPM
HOW CAN I FIND TRUE LOVE
THE DELL-VIKINGS
FB-205

FLIP
RECORDS, INC.
HOLLYWOOD CALIFORNIA
45-303
THIS PARADISE
THE DEL-AIRES

FLIP
RECORDS, INC.
HOLLYWOOD CALIFORNIA
45-315
A CASUAL LOOK
THE SIX TEENS

GEE
45 RPM
45 RPM
HARLEM NOCTURN

GEE
45 RPM
45 RPM

GEE
WHEN I FOUND YOU
THE HEARTBEATS
BARBARA-ANN
THE REGENTS
G-1065
45 RPM
GEE RECORDS
A DIVISION OF ROULETTE RECORDS INC.
GONE
45 RPM
45 RPM
Gone 5002
Vocal
DARLING
THE DUBS
GONE
records
Gone 5011
Vocal
COULD THIS BE MAGIC
THE DUBS
GONE
records
Gone 5121
45 RPM
SHE'S EVERYTHING (I WANTED YOU TO BE)
RAL DONNER
Gordy
DANCING IN THE STREET
MARTHA & THE VANDELLAS
ALL I NEED
G-7061
GORDY
THE TEMPTATIONS
Herald
45 RPM
45 RPM
PARADISE HILL
THE EMBERS
with
VI HAMILTON TRIO
410
Herald
45 RPM
45 RPM
STORY UNTOLD
THE NUTMEGS
HERALD
45RPM
LET'S MOVE
LIGHTNIN HOPKINS
H-542
HERALD
45 RPM
MIXED-UP, SHOOK-UP, GIRL
PATTY & THE EMBLEMS
H-590
HULL
RECORDS
45 RPM
45 RPM
Vocal
CRAZY FOR YOU
THE HEARTBEATS
H-711

HULL
RECORDS
HURRY HOME BABY
THE HEARTBEATS
45-H-713
HULL
A THOUSAND MILES AWAY
45-H-720
HULL
RECORDS
DADDY'S HOME
SHEP AND THE
LIMELITES
HULL
IT'S ALL OVER NOW
SHEP AND THE
LIMELITES
45-H-757
IMPERIAL
45-5262
DON'T LEAVE ME THIS WAY
FATS DOMINO
IMPERIAL
X5348
AIN'T IT A SHAME
FATS DOMINO
IMPERIAL
X5407
BLUEBERRY HILL
FATS DOMINO
IMPERIAL
X5675
DON'T COME KNOCKIN'
FATS DOMINO
JAMIE
1033
TRULY
MARIAN CARUSO
JAMIE
RECORDS
45 R.P.M.
1039
STRAWBERRY STOMP
ROBERT BYRD
AND ORCHESTRA
JAMIE
RECORDS
RAMROD
DUANE EDDY
Jamie
45 R.P.M.
1117
DETOUR
DUANE EDDY

BECAUSE THEY'RE YOUNG
Jamie
DUANE EDDY
LOUIE LOUIE
Jerden
THE KINGSMEN
712
Josie
SPEEDOO
THE CADILLACS
Josie
DO YOU WANT TO DANCE
BOBBY FREEMAN
Josie
THAT'S HOW MUCH I LOVE YOU
J. FRANK WILSON and THE CAVALIERS
Jubilee
LONELY CHRISTMAS
THE ORIOLES
Jubilee
I UNDERSTAND JUST HOW YOU FEEL
THE FOUR TUNES
Jubilee
POOR BOY
THE ROYALTONES
KING
THE DEATH OF HANK WILLIAMS
JACK CARDWELL
KING
MIRACLE OF LOVE
THE "5" ROYALES
KING
LOOK AT LITTLE SISTER
HANK BALLARD AND THE MIDNIGHTERS
KING
LONELY RAIN
THE MASCOTS

LEGRAND
RECORDS
"PLEASE FORGIVE ME"
LEGRAND
RECORDS
QUARTER TO THREE
U.S. BONDS
M-G-M
45 R.P.M.
K12677
IT'S ONLY MAKE BELIEVE
M-G-M
K13008
RESPECTABLE
THE CHANTS
Mercury
ONE IN A MILLION
THE PLATTERS
MERCURY RECORD CORPORATION, MADE IN U.S.A.
Mercury
LITTLE DARLIN'
THE DIAMONDS
MERCURY RECORD CORPORATION, MADE IN U.S.A.
milestone
RECORDS
I WANT LOVE
THE PARADONS
2003
milestone
RECORDS
45 RPM
LOVER'S ISLAND
THE BLUE JAYS
2008
Modern
Modern
RECORDS
45 RPM
hollywood
STRANDED IN THE JUNGLE
THE CADETS
MOTOWN
PLEASE FORGIVE ME
MARY WELLS
M-1003
MOTOWN
COME SEE ABOUT ME
THE SUPREMES

OKeh
45 RPM
4-7088
OKeh
45 RPM
4-7139
ZSP 52161
THE PONY
THE KID
"OKeh" Trade Mark Reg. U.S. Pat. Off. Marca Registrada, Made in U.S.A.
OKeh
45
RPM
4-7187
UM, UM, UM, UM, UM, UM
MAJOR LANCE
Old Town
RECORDS, INC.
45 RPM
45 RPM
GOOD LUCK DARLIN
5 CROWNS
Old Town
Record No.
O.T. 1012-45
45 R.P.M.
MY DEAR
THE SOLITAIRES
Old Town
UNBREAKABLE
45 R.P.M.
RECORD NO.
OT 1014
THE WEDDING
THE SOLITAIRES
Old Town
UNBREAKABLE
45 R.P.M.
RECORD NO.
1047
WE BELONG TOGETHER
ROBERT & JOHNNY
Old Town
RECORDS
Maureen Music
Record No.
1062
SO FINE
THE FIESTAS
OLD
TOWN
Publisher
Maureen Music Inc.
BMI
1133
NEVER
THE EARLS
ORIGINAL SOUND
RECORD CO.
TEEN BEAT
SANDY NELSON
ORIGINAL SOUND
COME ON IN
THE MUSIC MACHINE
Philles
RECORDS
UPTOWN
THE CRYSTALS
102

THE CRYSTALS
PHILLES RECORDS
BROTHER JULIUS
115
PHILLES RECORDS, A DIVISION OF PHIL SPECTOR PRODUCTIONS

THE CRYSTALS
PHILLES RECORDS
THEN HE KISSED ME
115

PROMO
RECORDS
45 R.P.M.
P-1002
A MILLION TO ONE
JIMMY CHARLES

RAMA
45 RPM
45 RPM
GEE
THE CROWS

RAMA
45 RPM
45 RPM
TWENTY MINUTES
(BEFORE THE HOUR)
THE VALENTINES

RCA VICTOR
47-6870
45 R.P.M.
ALL SHOOK UP
ELVIS PRESLEY

RIBBON

RIBBON
45-6911
ONLY THEN
SCOTT BROS.

Roulette

ROULETTE

Roulette

ROULETTE
JOEY DEE & the STARLITERS

ROULETTE
45 RPM
ALL THAT GLITTERS ISN'T GOLD
LOU CHRISTIE
ROULETTE
45 RPM
RIP VAN WINKLE
THE DEVOTIONS
RPM
NO MORE DOGGIN'
ROSCOE GORDON
RPM
RECORDS
EDDIE MY LOVE
THE TEEN QUEENS
RUST
RECORDS
DENISE
RANDY AND THE RAINBOWS
SAVOY
SUGAR WOOGA
THE THREE PLAYMATES
SAVOY
45 R.P.M.
STEP UP AND RESCUE ME
FAYE ADAMS
1606
SHAD
5002
WHO'S THAT KNOCKING
THE GENIES
SHAD
5013
RIOT IN ROOM 3C
THE KNOCKOUTS
Singular
SOMETIMES
DANNY AND THE JUNIORS
S-711
SNAP
RECORDS
102-A
HANKY PANKY
THE SHONDELLS
SPARK
RECORD CO.
WRAP IT UP

SPARK
RECORD CO.
MIDNIGHT SPECIAL
SPARK
RECORD CO
SMOKEY JOE'S CAFE
THE ROBINS
122-45
Specialty
45 R.P.M.
NITE OWL
TONY ALLEN
Specialty
BABY FACE
LITTLE RICHARD
SUN
GOLD COLD HEART
JERRY LEE LEWIS
Swan
CLICK-CLACK
DICKEY DOO
Swan
DON'T DROP OUT
"WHO DO YOU LOVE"
THE SAPPHIRES
S-4162-W
TAMLA
SHOP AROUND
THE MIRACLES
YOU'VE BEEN A LONG TIME COMING
MARVIN GAYE
TAMLA
IT TAKES TWO
MARVIN GAYE &
KIM WESTON
TIARA
MY BABY'S COMIN' HOME
RUTH McFADDEN
SAMMY LOWE
TOLLIE
RECORDS
LOVE ME DO
THE BEATLES

Trommers
THERE'S A MOON OUT TONIGHT
THE CAPRIS
VALMOR
PLEASE LOVE ME FOREVER
CATHY JEAN
VALMOR.
"BAND OF GOLD"
THE ROOMATES
A DIVISION OF COUNTESS INTERNATIONAL
Vee-Jay RECORDS
WHY DID SHE GO
THE MAGNIFICENTS
VJ 183
Vee-Jay RECORDS
BUS FARE HOME
THE SPANIELS
VJ 350
VEE JAY
MISERY
TASTE OF HONEY
THE BEATLES
VJ
VEE JAY RECORDS
PLEASE, PLEASE ME
THE BEATLES
DO YOU WANT TO KNOW A SECRET
THE BEATLES
VJ 587
VEE JAY
LITTLE BOY (In Grown Up Clothes)
THE FOUR SEASONS
WINLEY
RECORDS
45 R.P.M.
215 A
FLORENCE
THE PARAGONS
WINLEY
RECORDS
45 R.P.M.
ZOOM-ZOOM ZOOM
THE COLLEGIANS
WINLEY
RECORDS
45 R.P.M.
WIN 250 B
JUST A MEMORY
THE PARAGONS
MACK STARR

1100 series — maroon label or red label.

1500 — begins maroon, red or blue label.

REPRODUCTIONS

726	**Robins**	If I Didn't Love You So (Original unknown on 45 RPM)
738	**Robins**	Our Romance Is Gone (Original unknown on 45 RPM)
769	**Four Buddies**	I Will Wait
823	**Four Buddies**	Simply Say Goodbye
825	**Marshall Bros.**	Who'll Be The Fool From Now On (Original first press unknown on 45 RPM)
833	**Marshall Bros.**	Why Make A Fool Out Of Me
1508	**Jive Bombers**	Bad Boy

SHAD

Shad was another very small label only having a total of 21 releases and the two label styles detailed below.

SPECIFICS

5001 thru 5007 — pink label.

5011 — begins blue and white label.

REPRODUCTIONS

None.

SINGULAR

The major record of collector interest on Singular is "At The Hop" by Danny And The Juniors. The reproductions are easy to spot since the label color is incorrect. The original label is blue. Second pressings are not so easy to spot because the difference is in the recording. On first presses you can hear the count before the music starts (turn up the volume). Other popular recordings by the same group were never issued on Singular, and are obviously fake.

REPRODUCTIONS

711 Danny And The Juniors At The Hop

SNAP

Snap 102, "Hanky Panky" by the Shondells, deserves some explanation because of the lack of information among collectors, and a number of reproductions exist. The original first press of this recording does not have Dist. Nationally by Red Fox on the bottom of the label. These are all second press and about 100,000 were produced. All known reproductions are of the second pressing and should be of little consequence. Later about 10,000 copies were issued on Red Fox and finally Roulette. It is interesting to note that all legitimate copies on Snap (1st and 2nd press) are slightly slower than later pressings or counterfeits. A few very scarce legitimate copies exist on Atlantic also.

REPRODUCTIONS

102 Shondells Hanky Panky

SPARK

SPECIFICS

101 thru 108 — red with silver top.

109 — blue label.

110 thru 119 — red label with silver print.

120 — begins yellow and black label.

REPRODUCTIONS

103	Robins	Riot In Cell Block #9
104	Honey Bears	It's A Miracle
107	Robins	Framed
110	Robins	Whadaya Want
111	Honey Bears	I Shall Not Fail

SPECIALTY

The reissues on Specialty can be quite a problem because of the label similarity and the fact that the original dead wax information is identical. The most recent reissues can be detected by the rolled edge at the lead in groove, the originals are flat. In some cases there is information on the label pertaining to an LP that did not originally appear. The wax of most of the originals had somewhat of a used appearance even when new. The prefix 45-SP was used extensively in the dead wax.

SPECIFICS

400 thru 607 — yellow and white label, thin yellow line.

606 — begins yellow and white label without the thin yellow line.

REPRODUCTIONS

423	Four Flames	Wheel Of Fortune
461	Five Notes	Thrill Me Baby
472	Metronomes	She's Gone
548	Twilighters	It's True
572	Little Richard	Long Tall Sally
577	Zephyrs	A Foolish Fool

SUN

Sun, as you can see below, is one of the most heavily reproduced labels. A large majority of these are extremely good. Hopefully an awareness of what has been reproduced will make you more critical in any dealings with these records. Certain facts do apply to the label in general, and should be of some help in making a determination. Later Sun reissues have a label design somewhat different than that pictured in the photo section. Elvis Presley records with a shiny label are reproductions. Some originals had small circles in the shape of a triangle beneath the label that you could feel.

REPRODUCTIONS

175	Johnny London	Drivin' Slow (Original unknown on 45 RPM)
177	Handy Jackson	Got My Application Baby (Original unknown on 45 RPM)
178	Joe Hill Louis	She May Be Yours (Original unknown on 45 RPM)
179	Willie Nix	Baker Shop Boogie
180	Jimmy & Walter	Easy
181	Rufus Thomas	Bear Cat
183	D. A. Hunt	Lonesome Old Me (Original unknown on 45 RPM)
184	Memphis Marainey	Call Me Anything
185	Jimmy DeBarry	Take A Little Chance
186	Prisonaires	Just Walkin' In The Rain
187	Little Jr. Parker	Feeling Good
188	Rufus Thomas	Tiger Man
189	Prisonaires	My God Is Real
191	Prisonaires	A Prisoner's Prayer
193	Doctor Ross	Come Back Baby
194	Little Milton	Beggin' My Baby
195	Billy Emerson	No Teasin' Around
196	Hot Shot Love	Wolf Call Boogie
197	Earl Peterson	Boogie Blues
199	James Cotton	My Baby

200	Little Milton	If You Love Me
203	Billy Emerson	The Woodchuck
204	Raymond Hill	Bourbon Street Jump
205	Harmonica Frank	Rockin' Chair Boogie
206	James Cotton	Cotton Crop Blues
207	Prisonaires	There Is Love In You
208	Buddy Cunningham	Why Do I Cry
209	Elvis Presley	That's All Right
210	Elvis Presley	Good Rockin' Tonight
211	M. Yelvington	Drinkin' Wine
212	Doctor Ross	The Boogie Disease
213	Jones Bros.	Every Night (Original unknown on 45 RPM)
215	Elvis Presley	Milk Cow Blues Boogie
217	Elvis Presley	Baby Let's Play House
220	Little Milton	Lookin' For My Baby
222	Five Tinos	Sitting By My Window
223	Elvis Presley	Mystery Train
224	Carl Perkins	Gone Gone Gone
225	Slim Rhodes	House Of Sin
226	Eddie Snow	Ain't That Right
231	Charlie Feathers	Defrost Your Heart
234	Carl Perkins	Blue Suede Shoes
236	Jimmy Haggett	No More No More
241	Johnny Cash	I Walk The Line
242	Roy Orbison	Ooby Dooby
245	Billy Riley	Rock With Me Baby
247	Sonny Burgess	Red Headed Woman
254	Ray Harris	Come On Little Mama
255	Miller Sisters	Ten Cats Down
260	Billy Riley	Flying Saucers Rock & Roll
267	Jerry Lee Lewis	Whole Lotta Shakin' Going On
272	Ray Harris	Greenback Dollar
281	Jerry Lee Lewis	Great Balls Of Fire
293	Sunrays	Love Is A Stranger
300	Tommy Blake	I Dig You Baby
304	Sonny Burgess	Itchy
322	Billy Riley	Got The Water Boiling

SWAN

Swan used two basic label styles with minor variations on each. Both the black and the white label appeared with or without Don't Drop Out in the upper left. Blue print was also used on the white label as well as the more common red/maroon. Beware, there are reproductions on the Swan label that are machine stamped. Machine stamped originals past number 4053 also have Reco Art Phila stamped in the wax.

SPECIFICS

4001 thru 4129 — white label without Don't Drop Out.

4130 — begins white or black label, with or without Don't Drop Out, blue (scarce) or red/maroon print.

REPRODUCTIONS

4024	**Don Wayne**	Head Over Heels In Love
4031	**Freddy Cannon**	Talahassie Lassie
4043	**Freddy Cannon**	Way Down Yonder In New Orleans
4106	**Freddy Cannon**	Palisades Park
4152	**Beatles**	She Loves You (reproduced on the white label)
4182	**Beatles**	Sie Liebt Dich (reproduced on the label with She Loves You alongside)

TAMLA

SPECIFICS

101, 102, 54024 thru 54044 — yellow label, Tamla written vertically.

54044 thru 54140 — yellow label, globe and record at the top.

54141 — begins yellow and brown label.

REPRODUCTIONS

Many of the Tamla reproductions have a drill hole through the label.

54034	Miracles	Shop Around
54046	Marvelettes	Please Mr. Postman
54048	Miracles	Everybody's Gotta Pay Some Dues
54053	Miracles	What's So Good About Goodbye
54073	Miracles	You've Really Got A Hold On Me
54077	Marvelettes	Forever
54080	Stevie Wonder	Fingertips
54083	Miracles	Mickey's Monkey
54102	Miracles	That's What Love Is Made Of
54108	Stevie Wonder	Tears In Vain
54118	Miracles	Tracks Of My Tears
54124	Stevie Wonder	Uptight
54127	Miracles	Going To A Go Go
54176	Marvin Gaye	I Heard It Through The Grapevine

TIARA

One reproduction appears on the black Tiara label, "I Met Him On A Sunday" by the Shirelles. This record is easily detectable since the reproduction incorrectly shows the record number as 6100.

REPRODUCTIONS

6112	Shirelles	I Met Him On A Sunday

TOLLIE

TOLLIE had a tremendous amount of label variations and not all of these are pictured in the photo section. The two Beatle records, although produced on many variations of black or yellow, have been counterfeited on the yellow "box" style. Originals of "Twist and Shout" can be distinguished by the machine stamped MR with a circle around it located in the dead wax. The "Love Me Do" originals will have Audio Matrix machine stamped in the dead wax.

REPRODUCTIONS

9001	**Beatles**	Twist And Shout
9008	**Beatles**	Love Me Do

TROMMERS

Information on Trommers is included because of the unusually high value placed on "There's A Moon Out Tonight" by the Capris. The value is considered high in light of the fact that this record is a reissue that was pressed in 1966. The record actually appeared on three other labels prior to being issued on Trommers. Planet was the original label, Old Town was the popular label, and Lost Nite is the first reissue label. The Trommers label was either orange or pale blue.

VALMOR

The Valmor label was small in terms of number of releases and seemed to be dedicated to issuing Roommates records. A red label was used up to record 009 and should have a large V to be considered first press. Beyond this point the label changed to black with yellow print. Yellow labels are all second presses.

REPRODUCTIONS

None.

VEE JAY

SPECIFICS

100 thru 285 — maroon label with thin silver ring.

286 thru 353 — maroon label with thick silver ring.

354 — begins primarily black with a tremendous variation in style, some maroon.

REPRODUCTIONS

129	**Five Echos**	I Really Do
134	**Dells**	Tell The World
138	**Rhythm Aces**	Whisper To Me
156	**Five Echos**	Fool's Prayer
166	**Dells**	Dreams Of Contentment
173	**Kool Gents**	This Is The Night
184	**High Lighters**	Hello Dear
190	**Five Echos**	Pledging To You
207	**Kool Gents**	You Know
228	**Orioles**	For All We Know
263	**El Dorados**	Three Reasons Why
288	**Deltones**	Early Morning Rock
291	**Leonard Carbo**	So Tired
302	**El Dorados**	Lights Are Low
522	**Beatles**	From Me To You

WINLEY

Winley began issuing records in 1956 with number 212, and the series ended many years later with number 267. The first release, by the Duponts, was on a blue label. Reissues have the name WINLEY and some of the title lines in a larger, and more of a bold print style, than those shown and listed below.

SPECIFICS

212 — blue label.

213 thru 220 — orange label, WINLEY in 3/16" print.

221 thru 249 — orange label, WINLEY in 1/4" print.

250 — begins the same as 249 with the addition of the address below WINLEY, although there are exceptions, such as 261 and 264, appearing without the address.

REPRODUCTIONS

None.

Index of Reproductions by Artist

NOTES

ANNA
ARCADE
BANDERA
BAYOU
BIG TOWN
BLAZE
BLUES BOYS KINGDOM
BRENT
CMP
CALVERT
CAPROCK
CHANT
CIMARRON
CLUB
COVER
DC
DAMON
DARL
DART
DIR
DIXIE
DREW BLAN
DUCHESS
DUNCAN
ECHO
FOX
FREEDOM
GLOBAL
GOLDBAND
HARVEY
121
HOLIDAY INN
HUNTER
INTRO
IVORY
JALO
JAN
LUCKY 4
LYNNE
METEOR
PEARL
PENTHOUSE
PINK
PRINCESS
RON
SAGE
SARGE
SELMA
SHARA
SILHOUTTE
SITTIN IN WITH
SOUND
STOMPER TIME
SUGAR HILL
TNT
TALENT
TEEN LIFE
TENNESSEE
TRUMPET
TURF
TWINSTAR
ULTRA
VALLEY
VICEROY
WAR CONN
WARRIOR
WAYSIDE
WESTPORT
WAIRLIN DISC
WILDCAT
ZYNN